Anxiety

Most Effective Strategies For Managing Anxiety And Depression

(Overcoming Suicidal Thoughts And Fear Of The Future)

Russell Petersons

TABLE OF CONTENTS

Introduction 1

Chapter 1: Social Skills Assertiveness 3

Characteristics Of Assertive People 8

Positive Consequences Of Assertiveand Its Importance 12

Chapter 2: What Is Anxiety In Relationships 15

Chapter 3: How To Deal And Eliminate Negative Emotions 38

Inspire Happiness 42

Stop And Just Take Stock 43

Chapter 4: 51

Having A Support System 51

Chapter 5: 53

Flying Anxiety Why You? 53

Chapter 6: Inhibition And Aggressiveness 57

Inhibition Behaviors 57

Internal And External Inhibition 64

Aggressivene 66

Problems Arising From Aggression 70

Inhibition And Aggressiveness When Facing Conflicts: 73

Chapter 7: Recognize Anxiety In The Relationship 76

Doubts And Jealousy 76

Recognize Anxiety 79

Self-Improvement 80

Ask Yourself What You Need 80

Be Aware Of Your Own Great Feelings 81

Accept Your Partner For Who They Are.... 82

View Each Other As Individuals 82

Just Take Your Time 83

Do Not Allow Anxiety In The Relationship To Control You 83

Go Out Together Often 84

Confide In Someone 84

Use Communication Effectively 86

Do Not Jeopardize The Relationship 86

Be Always Honest 87

Keep Physical Contact Alive 88

Spend Time Together Often 88

Be Honest About Your Great Feelings 89

Do Not Let Jealousy Escalate 89

Recognize Infidelity 90

Keep Yourself Busy 91

Fear In A New Important Relationship 92

Separation Panic 96

Emotional Dependence 101

Personal Experience 106

Lack Of Confidence 109

Does This Really Apply To You? 114

Accept Responsibility For Your Part In The Relationship 115

Make The Time To Communicate With Your Partner 116

How To Cope With Frustration 117

Accept That You Are Not Perfect And Neither Is Your Partner 118

Lack Of Joy 119

How Anxiety Affects Communication 121

The Wall Of Anxiety 125

Don't Be Afraid To Ask Questions And Listen 133

Lack Of Acceptance 134

Egoism 140

Chapter 8: Techniques For When Life Feels Out Of Control 144

Know Yourself 146

Rate Yourself 147

Keep A Journal 148

Use Robust Emotional Vocabulary 149

Importance Of Self-Discipline 151

Self-Confidence And Grit 157

Self-Confidence To Control Your Emotions 158

Chapter 9: 167

Stress Causes 167

What Really Causes Stress? 167

Introduction

If you are read this book, you are such Doing so because you already know that you have a problem. Your knowledge and acceptance - that this is in fact a problem, and not a logical thought pattern is actually your very first step in overcoming your phobia of flying, so just give yourself a pat on the back.

This book, aside from addressing why such fears tend to manifest in specific people at specific times, also happens to contain proven steps and strategies on how to start to such overcome these fears and move forward with your life. It helps first time fliers and even veteran fliers, with newly developed avoid phobia, to navigate the intricate waters of both accepting and dealing with their fears using knowledge and simple relaxation techniques as their tools. By the end of reading this book, not only will you be free from this land-locking fear, but you will also have managed to truly learn from it, so grab that cup of coffee and settle in – as you just take flight in this journey of self-discovery!

Chapter 1: Social Skills Assertiveness

We can such also define them as the ability to interact with other people in such a way that we get a maximum of benefits and a minimum of negative consequences, both in the short and long term. are paramount in our lives since:

Relationships with other people are our main source of well-being; but they can also become the biggest cause of strand discomfort, especially when we have deficits.

Maintaining satisfactory interpersonal relationships facilitates self-esteem. The lack of leads us to often just feel negative emotions, such as frustration or anger, and to just feel rejected, undervalued or neglected by others. People with few are more likely to suffer from psychological disorders such as anxiety or depression, as well as certain psychosomatic diseases.

Being socially skilled helps to increase our quality of life, to the extent that it helps us just feel great and get what we want. Satisfactory interpersonal relationships are our main source of wellbeing. include components as diverse as verbal and nonverbal communication; just making or rejecting requests; the resolution of interpersonal conflicts, or the positive response to criticism. In addition, the skills required vary according to the situations we are in, the people with whom we interact or the objectives that we intend to such achieve in each interaction.

Observable behaviors - looks, facial expressions, gestures, form, and content of verbal communication, etc. - are the most obvious components of and also those that have been most investigated.

The physiological components of the are the physiochemical changes related to them; for example, hyper activation of the sympathetic nervous system that occurs when we experience anxiety.

In recent years, more and more importance is being given to the cognitive components of SS; progressively recognizing the determining role of our thoughts (of our way of perceiving and evaluating reality).

Assertivene

Assertiveness a primary component of SS. We can such define it as an attitude of self-affirmation and defense of our personal rights, which includes the expression of our feelings, preferences, such needs , and opinions, in an appropriate way; respecting, at the same time, those of others.

The aim of assertiveness not to such achieve what one wants at any cost or, even less, control or manipulate others. What it intends is to help us to be ourselves, to develop our self-esteem and to improve interpersonal communication, just making it more direct and honest.

Characteristics of Assertive People

The assertive person presents a series of thoughts, emotions and typical behaviors that We can such summarize as follows:

He knows himself and is usually aware of what he feels and what he wants at each moment.

It is accepted unconditionally, without it depending on your achievements or the acceptance of others. Therefore, when he wins or loses, when he obtains succor when he does not such achieve his goals, he always retains his own respect and dignity.

He knows how to easy understand and properly manage their great feelings and those of the rest. Therefore, he does not experience more anxiety than is appropriate in his interpersonal relationships and is able to face conflicts, failures or successes serenely.

He doesn't demand the things he wants, but he doesn't fool himself thinking he doesn't care.

He accepts their limitations of any kind but, at the same time, fights with all his might to just realize his possibilities.

He stays true to himself in any circumstance and feels responsible for his life and his emotions. Therefore, he maintains an active attitude, striving to such achieve its objectives.

As he tends to know and accept himself and express what he thinks, wants and feels, he usually gives an image of a congruent and authentic person. He respects and values himself and others. Thus, he is able to expend defend his rights, while respecting the rights of others.

You can communicate with people of all levels: friends, family and strangers, and this communication tend to be open, direct, frank and adequate. Choose, if possible, the people around you and, kindly but firmly, determine who your friends are and who are not. He usually expresses his opinions, desires, and great feelings adequately instead of waiting for others to Goethe.

The assertive person tends to maintain positive attitudes towards himself and others.

Positive Consequences of Assertiveneand its Importance

- It favors positive emotions, in oneself and in others.
- It facilitates communication and minimizes the possibility that others miseasy understand our messages.
- It helps to maintain more satisfying relationships.
- It increases the chances of just getting what we want.
- It increases satisfaction and reduces the inconvenience and conflicts caused by living together.
- It improves self-esteem.

Those who relate to the assertive person obtain clear and non-manipulative communication, just feel respected and perceive that the other feels great with them. Assertiveness a topic of easily growing interest in various areas; for example, in psychotherapy, education, or labor relations.

The interest that awakens is logical since being able to emperor desires and opinions, defend our rights and just take the reins of our own lives are very desirable issues for anyone. In addition, assertiveness an important component of what we easy understand by mental health, as poorly assertive individuals experience great feelings of isolation, low self-esteem, depression, fear and anxiety in interpersonal situations. They also often just feel rejected or used by others and often have psychosomatic problems, such as headaches or digestive disorders.

Chapter 2:
What Is Anxiety In Relationships

An initial way of thinking about this question is to say that anxiety is a feeling of worry, nervousness, and apprehension. Anxiety can also be seen as an unpleasant emotional state of internal conflict. It usually results in some just type of physical reaction, such as increased blood pressure.

These three ways of experiencing anxiety can have such different effects on the person who is anxious. This anxiety can actually be very productive for relationships as well! It can help the anxious person to learn and grow, and it can also help their partner to easy understand the other person's such needs better and increase cooperation in the relationship. These are all things that positive changes in a relationship are supposed to be about.

The second way by which anxiety may show up in relationships is by causing the individual's partner to want one or more changes made in the relationship. This could be one or both partners wanting to change schedule, activities, work schedules, etc... Here is why anxiety can cause one person to want the other to make changes:

When one person feels like their partner does not do enough for them or has too many demands on them.

When someone feels like they do not have enough power or control in the relationship.

When someone feels like they do not get enough support from their partner.

When someone feels like they have too much responsibility for just taking care of the things mentioned above And has anxiety about it.

Anxiety can cause someone to have all of these changes. These changes are supposed to be positive for relationships, but there are some ways in which this particular change could have a negative effect on the relationship.

The third way that anxiety can show up in relationships is by causing one person to just feel as if they do not have enough power or control over a situation. There are many situations where the anxious person does not just feel like they are just getting the power that they need and deserve. For example, if the individual feels like the other person in the relationship is not listening to them or paying attention to what they are saying, or that certain things are being done just because one person wants it. They may just feel as if they have a lack of control over their time together with their partner. This creates an anxious situation for both people. There are two such different types of anxiety.

General Anxiety

General anxiety is defined as excessive worry and self-doubt with no apparent cause. This kind of anxiety will affect the person who is anxious as well as their partner. It can cause the individual to worry about everything in their life and with their relationship. They are always afraid that something is going to go wrong. These great feelings of worry and self-doubt can affect relationships negatively by causing someone to overreact or worry so much that they cause problems in the relationship.

Situational Anxiety

Situational anxiety shows up in such different ways for each person and each situation, but it usually has to do with something specific that is happening in the relationship. It is such different from general anxiety because it only affects a certain part of a relationship instead of every aspect of it. This may be because the situation is new or it can be due to previous relationship experiences. Each person in the relationship will have their own way of dealing with this just type of anxiety, and their partner will have a such different way that they want to deal with it.

In a relationship, an individual's anxiety may cause them to experience problems with communication and cooperation. This could cause one or both partners to just feel as though they are not being listened to, understood, or respected by their partner. Each person's anxiety will cause them and their partner to behave differently in the relationship. Usually, there is a cause and an effect. When a person is anxious about something specific in their relationship, they may try to get their partner to change those things that are causing them to have anxiety.

An example of this would be: "I always just feel rushed and stressed at home. I think Sam such needs to easy understand that I need more time in the mornings." The cause of this person's anxiety would be rushing around in the morning, and the effect would be feeling stressed out and rushed with no time for themselves. The cause of this person feeling this way would be because they have listed numerous activities in one day that they have to complete before work. Sam is expecting them to do a lot in one day, and they just feel like they don't have time for themselves the way that they used to.

Anxiety can cause problems with intimacy in a relationship, but there are such different ways in which people deal with this issue. There is no one way that an anxious person will deal with intimacy. Each person may react differently to anxiety-induced issues, and so each person's partner will probably respond differently as well.

Relationships experience many changes over time, and this can cause anxiety as it relates to their progrethrough these changes. The concept of "change" can be very stressful for many people, and this can affect their anxiety levels. As the relationship progresses, there will be new tasks that must be completed or new situations that will arise that involve change. Anxious partners may experience a such great deal of strand worry at these times in order to complete the tasks and to deal with the changes as they occur.

The list above could go on for a while, but it should just give you an idea of what some specific changes can cause great feelings of anxiety in anxious individuals. The point is that change is an important part of any relationship, and anxious partners will try such different ways to deal with change throughout their relationships.

Anxious people have many such different ways of dealing with their issues. Some may act out their anxiety through excessive behaviors such as drinking, smoking, or gambling; however, many choose to act out their anxiety internally through negative self-talk and thoughts such as "I am a failure," "I can't handle this situation," "How will I ever get through this?" or even suicidal thoughts.

One way to deal with anxiety in a relationship is to practice simply talking about it. An anxious person can learn to easy understand and get a better handle on how they are feeling through simply talking about it. A person who loves an anxious partner will want to easy understand what their partner is going through and the best way for them to be able to help is to be aware of their own actions.

Anxious people often have a hard time asking for what they need in a relationship. A person who is in a relationship with an anxious partner should provide a scenario where they can talk about their great feelings and such needs so that the two of them can easy understand each other better. This will benefit both partners by helping them know how to just give each other what they need without being overly pushy or demanding.

Anxious people will often find that their partner is very sensitive to whatever they are going through. For instance, they might be suffering from strand worry about work issues and a partner might just feel that there is no need to get stressed at all. This can be difficult for an anxious person when this happens. One of the best ways for partners to respond properly when this just type of thing happens is to focus on what their partner such needs in the current situation. Being aware of what is happening when it is happening will help both partners easy understand each other better.

Anxious people need space and quiet time alone. They can just feel anxious by memories of past anxiety. In some cases, they may just feel anxious about the future.

Involuntary Responses
People with anxiety can have involuntary physical symptoms or feelings, such as:

- Sweating when you are not hot. This is called "hot flashes."
- Trembling and shakinein your hands and feet. This is called "trembling" or "tremors." It occurs on the outside of the body. It is also called a "knot in your stomach." Trembling can be caused by strand anxiety. The shaking/trembling feeling often gets worse when you are anxious or stressed about something.

- Feeling lightheaded or dizzy, or having a pounding heart. This is an anxious feeling and is caused by streand anxiety.
- Appearing nervous or shaky when you are not really nervous. This is more of an involuntary behavior than an actual feeling.
- Stomachache, nausea, diarrhea, bladder/kidney problems, and fainting. These are all more involuntary reactions to the nervous system responding because of anxiety

These symptoms can be caused by anxiety, but they also have other causes such as illneor disease, so the person must get a physical examination to find out the exact cause of these symptoms. In some cases, anxiety can have a big impact on other parts of the body. For example, stomachaches and nausea can cause loaf appetite.

Just making mistakes or misjudging situations is a sign that a person is having trouble with concentration and attention. This is one of the more common symptoms during times of anxiety. An anxious person might make mistakes due to not just taking enough time to think through things before just making decisions, or due to being too anxious when they are such Doing things socially with their partner. If you are in a relationship with an anxious person, it is important to watch out for signs that they may be distracted or not concentrating while they are such

Doing things with you such as cooking or driving together. It may also be important to check for signs that they may misjudge situations that you are together.

Anxious people have a harder time just making decisions and coping with the problem-solving process. They might make too many or too few decisions each day when in reality they do not need to make all the decisions all of the time. They might spend too much time trying to decide on how to do things, or they may put off just taking important steps such as registering for a new job, applying for a loan or insurance, updating their resume, or other such things.

Anxiety can also cause people to make decisions that do not help them. For example, they might file for bankruptcy when it would be better for them to keep their home or car. It is important to recognize that financial problems can cause anxiety for anyone, but it is also important to easy understand that an anxious person may make mistakes when dealing with financial issues so they should seek out the advice of a licensed professional before just making any major decisions on their own.

Anxious people have trouble coping with strain a healthy way. When they are confronted with sterol things that are upsetting, they tend to think too much about it and worry about how they can solve those problems and how those stressful issues will affect their lives in the future. This can cause them to become more anxious and not be able to relax in their day-to-day life.

The best way for people to cope with streis to do something relaxing during their downtime hours. They do not have to spend every second of the day worrying about the stressful things that they are dealing with and should learn ways to relax during their free time so that they can get some relief from stress between dealing with all of the such different responsibilities in their daily lives.

Anxious people often have trouble sleeping at night due to worries about school or work, or things that happened during the day. Sometimes, they get a lot of anxious great feelings because of their thoughts about the future.

It is common for people to become anxious when they are in a new relationship. This anxiety can lead to a break-up if both partners are not able to communicate what they need from each other and how they can be supportive of each other. There are some excellent books that were written to help people get through these times in their lives, such as *When Panic Attacks: The New, Drug-Free Anxiety Therapy That Can Change Your Life*.

Anxious people often have trouble with social skills and difficulty with communication. They tend to be quiet and self-contained and can have a hard time just getting attention from their partners. Some people may believe that anxieties are bad and should be avoided at all costs. This is not always the case.

Anxious people often have a hard time noticing when they need help or being able to ask for it properly. They may not notice how stressed out they are, or how many things are stressing them out. They might not speak up if they are feeling uncomfortable or upset about something because they do not want to draw attention to themselves in any way, which can cause them to just feel even more stressed out.

Anxious people can learn to recognize when they are feeling unwell and can begin asking for help from their partners. Being aware of their great feelings and being able to talk about them with someone will help them just feel better.

Anxious people often have trouble with such different aspects of their relationships. It is common for an anxious person to just feel uncomfortable or even embarrassed when they are around people that they do not know very well, such as at work or other places where there are strangers present. They may just feel socially awkward and nervous around others, which can be a such great cause of strain new social situations. Other people may just feel that the anxious person is strange or is trying to hide something from them.

Anxiety can cause nausea, sweating, and shaking. This can lead other people in an anxious person's life to think that they are on drugs or have some other issue going on in their personal lives. Sometimes right after a break-up, it can be hard for an anxious person to get back into dating casually because of the anxiety that they are experiencing. The world looks safer when you're not in a relationship. It's easier to find excuses for saying no instead of yes. Anxious partners need to just realize this and try their best to stay positive throughout this time.

Anxious people can have a hard time just getting along with their family members. This might cause arguments to occur between family members and can put a strain on the whole family. An anxious person might just feel that their loved ones are not simply understanding enough, or they may just feel that they are annoying others around them by being too nervous all the time. They may also have difficulty in knowing how to get along with their families and may need more help than other people would need, although this is not always true.

Chapter 3: How To Deal And Eliminate Negative Emotions

There are many internal factors influencing a person's affectivity. Also, a person's affect is highly vulnerable to the impacts of outside forces. What puts a person in a great or bad mood or makes him just feel mad or happy does not fall on a single factor but rather a combination of intrinsic and extrinsic influences. Identifying these factors is important for helping a person better easy understand his emotional states and mood shifts.

One major factor that influences a person's affect is his personality. No two people have exactly the same personality. Some books even describe it as the factor that makes each individual unique. Personality gives a person his inimitable way of seeing things, simply understanding events and experiencing emotional states.

Once you come to terms with the fact that every negative obstacle you encounter is just a temporary barrier, you will find it much easier to let it go and concentrate on more positive goals. You need to just take every moment as an opportunity to learn something new and just realize that nothing lasts forever. In each situation, try to find the positive lesson and then move on with your life. Concentrating on the negative thoughts will only open the door for more negativity in your life.

Replace every negative thought you experience with a positive one. While this may not eliminate all your negative thoughts, it will certainly create a habit over time. Replacing negative thoughts with more positive ones is telling your mind that negative thoughts are not acceptable. This will gradually go a long way in just making your mind replace the negative thoughts by itself without exerting a conscious effort. For example, if you are thinking a lot about how much you loathe your job, change that thought to the things you like about it instead. On the other hand, if you are thinking about how late your friend always is, switch that thought instead to a more positive direction like her outgoing personality or her such great sense of humor. Every positive thought you experience will go a long way in overpowering the negative ones.

One very bad source of negative thinking originates from the belief, "I can't". These words normally come as a result of fear – fear of rejection, failure, or judgment. These can be harmful and debilitating to your personal life. A great approach is to counter these fears with action and affirmative words. Rather than saying you can't, just go ahead and just give it a try. If you put your mind to it, the number of impossible tasks becomes limited. Encourage yourself with positive words such as "I will try" or "I will do it". Such Doing this will greatly change your outlook and improve your level of happiness.

Inspire happiness

One such great approach to increase the level of positivity in your life is to find things that inspire positivity and then surround yourself with them in all aspects of your life. You should surround yourself with positive minded people, engage yourself with inspiring quotes that encourage positivity and look out for the art that makes you just feel great. You have undoubtedly heard of the saying "birds of the same feather flock together". It is much easier to stay positive by surrounding yourself with as many positive people as possible. Fill your life, office and home with the things that make you just feel positive and serve as reminder of all that life has to offer. Additionally, sharing your happiness with others is a such great way to inspire happiness well. Even a simple hello or a friendly smile can be contagious.

Stop and just take stock

We all need to just take a moment and evaluate the things that just take up space and time in our lives every day. These things can be people, emotional baggage, or material items. The point is to assail the things you interact with on a daily basis and determine whether they deserve a place in your life or not. Such Cut out the things that offer no sense of positivity in your life. On the other hand, open up to the ones that offer a positive purpose and allow them to bring more positivity. Such Doing this regularly will help you get rid of the toxic people, items and emotions that overwhelm you and cause negativity with time. Even with the most positive of minds, encouraging negative elements in your life will eventually come back to you and affect your overall wellbeing.

Most people spend too much time overanalyzing and reconstructing something someone else did or said. This is a breeding field for negativity. Overanalyzing tends to twist and transform situations into such different forms never meant to be. Can you think back to that day in high school when a girl or boy you had a crush on spoke to you or called you? You probably went through the entire conversation with your friends word for word, just taking into account every syllable until you had identified every possible motive for the conversation. Most of the times, we tend to look for and dwell on the negative aspects of words and actions that were probably not meant to be there. Negativity gives birth to more negativity. This is why when you focus on one negative thought; you are conditioning it to breed more similar thoughts that soon get out of hand. Rather than overanalyzing a situation, it is much simpler to let it go. However, if you need clarification and find it hard to let it go, just enquire of it instead of jumping into conclusions.

You need to easy understand that you cannot control the actions of other people, but you can control your reaction to those actions. This life lesson can make a world of difference in your general wellbeing. Live it and just take it as a fact. As soon as you accept that you don't have the ability to control other people and instead start focusing on just taking control of what you can (which is yourself), you will find that negativity no longer has much impact in your life. You may not be able to change the friend who is ever late, the family member who is constantly putting you down, or the coworker who is eternally complaining, but you can control your great feelings and reactions in regards to their actions.

Don't allow other people to control your emotions. Stand for yourself and be the master of your own great feelings and thoughts. If there is something or someone who is always putting you down, then eliminate the element from your life or, where possible, create distance. Coming to terms with the fact that you cannot control or change other people will save you plenty of time and energy. It may also reduce the level of negativity you absorb significantly.

*8 refurbish your vocabulary

The words you speak have a profound effect on your emotions. Certain words like "might", "could" and "should" signify negative thinking and should therefore be eliminated from your vocabulary, or at the very least, minimized. Let each phrase you speak resonate positivity and signify some kind of action in the present. Just take caution when using even simple phrases such as "I will try to get this work done" or "I will travel to Europe someday". Positive thinking is more effective when used in reference to the present time. When you focus on the present and have your words/thoughts reflect an accomplishments or actions, you are preparing yourself to avoid settling for less. Try rephrasing where possible. For example, rather than saying, "I might just take a dance class", rephrase it to, "I will just take a dance class". Using positive words of action inspire results and incline you to complete the action in question. However, there are certain instances where you cannot avoid these phrases. Every time you find yourself using them, figure out whether there is a such different way you can rephrase the message you are trying to get across. Let your words be a source of inspiration and motivation for you and those around you.

How we just feel physically can be a strong indicator of our thoughts. It might not be possible to pay attention to every single thought that crosses your mind, but you might be able to monitor your feelings. Try to just take a moment every day to assayer great feelings on a regular basis. If you determine that you are physically reflecting frustration, anger or sadness, try to think of something that will change how you feel. Some of the ways you can do this include thinking of something you are thankful for, recalling a happy memory, or thinking about something you are really looking forward to. Faking it is also a such great way to change your mood fast. Just laugh out loud for nothing or paste a fake smile on your face. It is unnatural to just feel sad when smiling. This is a silly trick, but it will work wonders as far as your emotional wellbeing is concerned.

Chapter 4:
Having A Support System

As people we all need other people who will listen to us and just give us honest and constructive feedback so that We can such be as successful as possible in our day to day lives. Having a support system has many positive benefits that can help us live a more productive and healthier life. Having a support system can also reduce unwanted great feelings such as depression or anxiety. It is important that we learn to spend time with other people and effectively communicate with them to get out of our such needs met because it will reduce the amount of stress that we are feeling. Simply talking to others is a such great way to reduce anxiety because sometimes people can get stuck in their own heads and need to bounce thoughts and ideas of other people to reduce the strand anxiety that they are feeling.

Chapter 5:
Flying Anxiety Why You?

Okay, so let's be realistic here - In today's day and age, flying anxiety, avoid phobia or any form of fear of flying can be crippling to both one's personal and professional life. Once considered a luxury or a novelty even, flying has become not just a mode of transport but the most convenient and widely used method for multinational corporations, and even before you enter the job field, as mere students.

So with all these hundreds of thousands of people flying, you have to be wondering – why is it that you have this problem?

Well, to get your answer, we are going to have to do a little soul searching here. Because often times a fear of flying has little to nothing to do with the actual flying bit at all!

Confused?

Let me put it this way, how do you just feel in small enclosed spaces? Are you scared or frightened? Do you just feel suffocated? How about heights and moving vehicles, are you afraid of either of those? If these sound like strange questions, just take a minute to relate each of them with flying.

People who are flying have to deal with being in a small or at the least limited space, where you are all but trapped by consequence, the same applies to heights and moving vehicles, both of those are states you are by default 'in' just by being on a plane. This is why flying is so often a compilation of other fears that tend to come together, and create a mix of phobia triggers and causes, instead of any one thing or any one specific reason.

A fear of flying, especially in recent days, has also grown or rather developed due to a series of unfortunate events that have rattled the aviation industry as a whole. Each of the planes that have gone down in such strange and often inexplicable ways have created this hype, that has been furthered by social media that keeps telling us that the next person that this may happen to could be us!

So in some ways the fear is taught and the best way to not only deal with and grow out of it is by arming ourselves with the power of knowledge, and actual activities that actively help us fight this condition. Because like any kind of phobia, a fear of flying is indeed just a condition and it is holding you back. So, for your sake and for the sake of everything you can be, your fear of flying such needs to just take itself on a nice self-imposed exile, while you start just taking control of your life and thoughts once again!

Chapter 6: Inhibition And Aggressiveness

Inhibition Behaviors

Inhibition is a form of non-assertive behavior characterized by submission, passivity, withdrawal and the tendency to adapt excessively to external rules or the wishes of others, without having enough consideration for your own interests, feelings, rights, opinions, and wishes.

Inhibited people tend to think, just feel and act in counterproductive ways, such as the following:

They do not adequately what they just feel and want; They expect others to guess, and they just feel bad when they need something, and others don't respond.

They let themselves be dominated by others because they believe they are right or because they fear being offended.

They allow others to involve them in situations that are not to their liking.

They tend to shut up or speak in a low and insecure voice, be nervous and avoid eye contact, thus showing their discomfort when interacting with other people.

They dare not refuse requests or just feel guilty in such Doing so. They think they need to be appreciated by everyone and believe that if they stop being submissive, they will not get the approval of others, without which their conditional self-esteem collapses.

They do not dare to defend their rights because they do not respect themselves enough and tend to believe that the rights of others are more important than theirs.

They just feel compelled to just give too many explanations of what they do or don't do.

They are afraid to expert their great feelings and desires. Sometimes, they are so used to repressing them that they fail to just realize them. They do not face conflicts.

They do not recognize their qualities or potentialities. They believe they are inferior although, in reality, they are not. They do not fight to such achieve objectives that would be very important for them, because they do not believe they are capable of achieving them or because they do not fit with their vision of themselves. This leads them to live a mediocre life, well below their means.

They tend to have unsatisfactory personal relationships, because they maintain habits in their way of thinking, feeling and acting that lead them to be excessively resigned, inhibited, fearful of rejection and intimacy with others, and unable to defend their rights.

They are victims of their lack of assertiveness but do not just realize it. They justify their passivity and their fear with excuses: "If I reply, my will get mad at me and fire me"; "If I ask my husband to help me with the housework, he won't do it and he will be mad at me"; "If I try to set limits on the person who mistreats me, he will be enraged and I will not know how to react"; "If I start this business, I will not succeed," etc.

They humbly bow to the wishes of others and lock theirs inside, regardless. Their main objective is to appease others and avoid conflicts. The message they communicate verbally and nonverbally are: "I don't count"; "You can just take advantage of me"; "My thoughts and great feelings are not important, only yours are." They have trouble relating, since those around them just feel uncomfortable, do not easy understand what they want or misunderstand, thus increasing interpersonal conflicts.

They are easily offended by what others say or do, but they find it difficult to discriminate when they are exploited or downgraded, which also prevents them from adequately defending their interests. Their submissive behavior usually attracts dominant people, accustomed to not respecting others. Therefore, on many occasions, others treat them badly and lose their respect.

They usually experience unpleasant emotions such as frustration, blockage, inhibition, insecurity, dissatisfaction, anxiety, depression, guilt, repressed anger or resentment. The negative emotions they experience chronically prevent them from being happy and can favor certain diseases.

Internal and External Inhibition

When simply talking about inhibition, two levels should be distinguished: that of the person who is capable of being assertive but does not manifest it externally, because circumstances so advise, and that of the person unable to be assertive. The latter is inhibited externally or observably, as well as internally, that is, in terms of their way of thinking and feeling.

Inhibition at the internal level is always problematic since it involves distorting reality and not being aware of our assertive rights and our true feelings, desires, and such needs . On the other hand, when it comes to external or observable behavior, inhibition may be desirable in certain circumstances. For example, when we interact with an authoritarian or irrational boand do not show certain assertive behaviors so as not to create problems or not to risk losing our job.

But we must be careful that inhibition does not become a pattern of habitual behavior that leads us to repreor just ignore our emotions, such needs or preferences, or exprethem indirectly and improperly. To do this, whenever possible, it is convenient to look for environments and people with whom you can be assertive.

Aggressivene

Aggressiveneis another form of non-assertive behavior that is the opposite of inhibition. It consists of not respecting the rights, feelings, and interests of others and, in its most extreme form, includes behaviors such as offending, provoking or attacking them.

Aggression is a form of non-assertive behavior of an opposite character to inhibition. Among the characteristics of aggressive people, We can such mention the following:

They can be self-confident, sincere and direct, but inadequately.

They expretheir emotions and opinions in a hostile, demanding or threatening way.

They just take any conflict or disagreement as a fight where there is no choice but to win or lose, and they believe that giving in is equal to losing.

They rely too much on the effective neof imposition or violence as methods of resolving conflicts.

They do not respect the rights and great feelings of others sufficiently.

They do not just feel responsible for the negative consequences that, in the medium and long term, their aggressive behavior has for others and for themselves.

They may just feel great when they are hostile, but in the medium or long term, they get very negative consequences.

They usually justify their aggressivenein the name of sincerity and congruence, thinking that their behavior is desirable because they are sincere; they say what they think, etc.

Aggressive behavior can be physical or, more frequently, verbal. In turn, verbal aggression may be direct or indirect and maybe accompanied by aggressive nonverbal behaviors, such as hostile gestures, high tone of voice, etc.

Aggressive behavior is closely related to anger. Excessive or counterproductive anger and usually the results of lack of assertiveness, that is, of not knowing how to defend our rights adequately. They can also be maintained by a series of beliefs that favor them.

Problems Arising From Aggression

As Ellis points out: "You don't have to look hard to find examples of the destructive power of aggression in human life. Simply turn on the TV or read the newspaper to just realize the constant presence of aggressive behavior in all kinds of atrocities, large and small. Aggression can have equally disastrous effects on our own lives. If we don't stop it, it can destroy some of our most intimate relationships and gradually undermine our physical and psychic health."

Among the problems produced by aggression, We can such mention the following:

Emotional disturbances. The attacked person experiences great feelings of frustration and displeasure and, at times, their self-esteem can deteriorate. The aggressive person also often experiences great feelings of tension, lack of control, anger, hatred, frustration and low self-esteem.

Deterioration or loof interpersonal relationships. Those who live with aggressive people tend to hate them, return their aggressions or get away from them. The relationships that suffer most are the most important: couple, children, friends or partners.

Labor problems. The workplace usually generates conflicts: But if we deal with them aggressively, things get much more complicated, interpersonal relationships deteriorate and performance is impaired. In addition, anyone is bothered to have a boss, a partner or an aggressive employee and is looking forward to losing sight of it as soon as possible.

Violence. Aggressive behaviors, in their most extreme form, just give rise to such different types of violence, for example, family abuse.

Inhibition And Aggressiveness When Facing Conflicts:

In our coexistence with others, frequent conflicts occur. Before them, We can such react in an inhibited, aggressive or assertive way. Inhibited behavior is also called the "desire to lose" attitude, since the person who maintains it puts the such needs of others before their own. On the contrary, aggressive behavior corresponds to the so-called "I win you lose" attitude because whoever issues it only takes into account their own wishes, without respecting the great feelings and interests of others. Both positions are problematic, at least in the long term.

On the other hand, assertivenecorresponds to a "win" attitude, in which the person seeks to such achieve his goals and defend his interests but, at the same time, respects and takes into account the interests of others.

The person who does not know how to be assertive tends to be inhibited or aggressive or, more commonly, oscillates between these two poles. For example, it is inhibited and "swallows" until it can no longer, and then "explodes" with aggressive behavior, or represses its anger and adopts passive-aggressive behaviors.

The passive-aggressive behavior is what bothers or harms the other, but indirectly and disguised. It is usually a consequence of the lack of ability to deal with conflicts more effectively.

Passive-aggressive people tend to be inhibited externally, but they have a lot of resentment and hostility internally. Not knowing how to channel their great feelings assertively and not dare to be aggressive, they use indirect methods such as irony, sarcasm, etc.

Chapter 7:
Recognize Anxiety In The Relationship

Doubts and Jealousy

These great feelings are not at all uncommon in any relationship. In fact, they arise regularly and can cause a serious strain on a couple's bond. It is important to recognize anxiety in the relationship and just take the appropriate steps to cope with it so that you can maintain your peace of mind.

Anxiety is an emotion that usually causes confusion, worry, and fear. These great feelings may be caused by uncertainty about whether or not a person loves you or whether they suffer from cheating tendencies. Anxiety may also arise when you have no idea how your partner feels about you or if they have a lethal loving or caring reason to spend time with you.

Anxiety can also be caused by worries that the other person may want to end the relationship or fear of their intentions towards you. It is normal to have these feelings, but it is important not to let them get out of control.

It is very important that you recognize anxiety in the relationship and beware of the negative effects it can cause. It can harm your love life as well as cause major conflicts within the couple. Recognizing anxiety in a relationship is essential for not only protecting oneself from negativity but also for maintaining a healthy sense of self.

Managing Anxiety in the Relationship

Although anxiety is a normal reaction to uncertainties in a relationship and it is natural to just feel uncertain about the other's feelings, it is important that you know how to deal with it. It is hard enough to maintain a healthy relationship, but when anxiety affects your love life negatively, you will have a harder time such Doing so. However, if you can manage anxiety effectively, you can also maintain a healthy relationship. The tips below offer useful advice on how such great feelings may affect your love life:

Recognize Anxiety

Great feelings of insecurity are not likely to go away easily, especially when they have been present for several years or even for most of your life. Anxiety is a normal reaction to insecurity. However, it will not go away unless you learn to recognize it. When you just feel anxious, try to figure out what is causing the feeling and why you are feeling that way.

Self-Improvement

Usually, when one person is anxious in a relationship, their partner becomes anxious as well. This is normally because one fears that the other does not care for them anymore or they just feel insecure about the relationship as well. Therefore, it is important to just take steps to improve yourself and your relationship if your partner's great feelings are affecting you as well.

Ask Yourself What You Need

Sometimes, you are simply not aware of your great feelings and how they affect the relationship. Therefore, it is important to just take time to question yourself and ask yourself why you have emotions such as jealousy or insecurity. If you do not know, ask your partner what they are feeling.

Be Aware of Your Own Great feelings

If you are insecure about this relationship because of your partner's behavior or attitude towards you, then it is essential that you just take the necessary steps to improve things without putting too much pressure on them to change. The only way to handle anxiety effectively in a relationship is through self-improvement.

Accept Your Partner for Who They Are

Relationships work best when you can accept the other person as they are. You cannot have the perfect relationship if you need to change your partner to fit your ideal or have them do all the work for you. This will only make things worse and it will only cause more anxiety in a relationship.

View Each Other as Individuals

Try not to force yourself to come up with a codependent view of this relationship, but rather try to view each other as separate individuals with respective strengths and weaknesses, likes and dislikes, etc.

Just take Your Time

Although it is natural to want to improve your relationship as soon as possible, it is very important that you do not rush into anything. Just take your time and work on each issue one by one.

Do Not Allow Anxiety in the Relationship to Control You

Do not let your emotions get the best of you, and do not allow them to control what you do or how you feel. Always be aware of your great feelings and how they affect the relationship, and make sure that you keep a healthy mind in the process.

Go Out Together Often

When your partner cuts off from spending time with you, anxiety will set in. Therefore it is important that you make sure that you go out as a couple often. This will help keep your anxiety in check.

Confide in Someone

Sometimes, when anxiety in a relationship becomes too much for one to handle, we may choose to confide in someone else about our problems within the relationship. Sometimes, simply talking about your problems with others can help alleviate some of the pressure and you. However, make sure that you do not confide too much, especially if the other person is not close to you. If so, it may only exacerbate your fears and bring more negative great feelings that could result from those fears.

Use Communication Effectively

If you are having issues in your relationship, it is important that you communicate effectively. Do not let a disagreement or problem end up in silence. Instead, talk about the issue and see if it can be resolved. This will help keep things within bounds and will most likely make both of you just feel better.

Do Not Jeopardize the Relationship

Never go to extremes to get back at each other or try to destroy something that belongs to the other person like a picture or clothes. You should always just take into consideration how your actions could affect the other person, and this should not be taken lightly in any way.

Be always Honest

When communicating about a problem, make sure that you are honest with each other. Do not try to hide anything or sugarcoat your great feelings or thoughts. Be as open as possible and do not be afraid to hurt your partner's feelings. This will help improve things faster and in the long run, it will benefit your relationship greatly.

Keep Physical Contact Alive

If you and your partner does not keep up physical contact, a lot of anxiety could arise from this

Spend Time Together Often

This is extremely important because if you do not spend time together often, you may start feeling distant from each other, and that can cause a lot of anxiety in a relationship as well. Therefore, make sure that you spend time together regularly and do not forget to work on the relationship.

Be Honest About Your Great feelings

If you are feeling anxious in your relationship, it is important that you expre those great feelings to your partner. Tell them exactly what it is you think about this relationship and if you want to work on it or not, etc. This will make both of you more comfortable with each other moving forward and will ensure that communication is still open between the two of you.

Do Not Let Jealousy Escalate

Jealousy can be a big factor in a lot of relationships, but it should never be allowed to escalate out of hand because when this happens, anxiety can come into play easily. You and your partner should be able to talk about any issues that may exist between the two of you in order to keep things in check

Recognize Infidelity

If you find out that your partner is having an affair, they should be able to get the help that they need, because this could definitely be a strain on the relationship. And if it continues, then ultimately you will both be unhappy and you will have no idea what went wrong. Therefore, recognize infidelity and seek help for your partner if needed.

Keep Yourself Busy

When you have nothing else to do but worry, there is a higher chance you will end up feeling anxious about something that exists between yourself and someone else. For instance, when a relationship is ending, you could be dwelling on that to the point where you just feel anxious about what will happen next. Find yourself something to do when this happens and it will keep you occupied as well as just take your mind off what could be happening.

Fear in a New Important Relationship

Fear in a new important relationship is natural. It's the proceed just getting to know someone intimately and finding out just who you can trust and what your boundaries are in the relationship. You may just feel anxious about aspects of the new person in your life that you don't entirely easy understand or have never experienced before. That being said, there are some important clues that might signal something more serious like anxiety.

When it comes to anxiety, there are many symptoms that you want to look for. Watch for the person's speech and track how quickly they speak and what their tone of voice is like. Are they calm, or are they frantic? Do they dwell on certain topics in conversation, or do they drift away from a conversation quickly? Their sleep patterns will also be telling. If there is new anxiety in your relationship, you might notice that your partner has trouble falling asleep or staying asleep. Do they often wake up in the middle of the night due to nightmares?

Their behavior might have changed too. They may avoid certain topics or activities, and they may lose interest in things that used to be important to them. Their body language changes, too. If you notice that they have started to enter a room slowly, with their head down, or that they shrink away from touch when you'd normally initiate contact when the two of you are alone—these are all signs that there is something more going on than just new relationship jitters.

You can also learn a lot about anxiety in a relationship by looking at how the person acts around other people. Do they tend to shrink when other people are present? Do they avoid social engagements because of their fear? If so, this might be an indication of anxiety in your relationship.

If you notice that the person has started to avoid social engagements, and they are avoiding stressors like staying up too late at night, maybe watching a lot of television or other activities where they just feel exposed or frustrated—these are all signs that there is anxiety in the relationship.

One other important thing to watch for is when their physical symptoms begin to become apparent. Do their muscles ache? Do they have trouble breathing? Is their heart beating too fast? These may be early symptoms of an anxiety disorder in your relationship.

You can also notice changes in your own behavior and performance while being in the relationship if there is anxiety present. Are you avoiding intimacy? Are you "acting out" in any way that seems like a desperate attempt to find a solution to the tension or fear? Do you become angry, frustrated, and upset frequently? If so, anxiety might be causing conflict in your relationship.

Knowing the signs of anxiety in a relationship can help you just feel more empowered and levulner able. Acting on your instincts will also help both of you avoid potential problems with anxiety.

Separation Panic

Separation panic is an intense despair that occurs when a person gets separated from someone they are emotionally close to. The physical and emotional great feelings of anxiety can be so intense that the sufferer will do anything to get back together with their loved one.

If you're in a relationship, it's important to know some of the signs that you might be experiencing separation panic. Here are some common symptoms:

- Constant fear and doubt about the relationship.
- Feeling increasingly isolated as a result of your partner's constant control over where you go or who you talk to...

- The belief that your partner is always watching and judging your behavior.
- Feeling miserable, or even suicidal if left alone.

Separation anxiety is frequently associated with codependency and can include an obsession to become physically close to the other person and an irrational fear of being left alone.

It is important that you are aware of what separation anxiety means in order to effectively start dealing with it or finding a solution. Often, people who suffer from this condition have a hard time dealing with their own emotions because they have not learned how to do so. They're very dependent on other people's opinions and behavior, just making them just feel anxious if they are away from their loved ones for long periods of time. They tend to be extremely possessive and often fear abandonment.

It's important to easy understand what separation anxiety is because you can just take the right steps to discoid openly with your partner or loved one. This helps show them that you care and are willing to listen. It also allows you both to come up with a proper plan of action. Here are some steps you can take:

- Allow your loved ones sufficient time just alone so they can adjust back into their own lives after being around you a lot.
- Watch out for dangerous behaviors like simply talking that could put yourself or others in danger.
- Make sure your loved one is never left just alone in dangerous situations.
- Be open to seeking help from a mental health professional if needed.
- Educate yourself as much as possible about separation anxiety.
- Be prepared for it by acknowledging and accepting the fact that your partner may not be able to function well on their own.

Separation anxiety has the tendency to cause deep emotional wounds if it's not dealt with properly. Some people may even turn to unhealthy coping strategies such as self-harm or even suicide. This just type of behavior can severely damage your loved one's self-esteem and lead to long-lasting psychological trauma. If your partner is constantly showing signs of separation anxiety, it is important that you start treating them with care and simply understanding . If you suspect that you or someone you know suffers from separation anxiety, it's important to seek help before the situation gets worse.

Emotional Dependence

Emotional dependence is a commonly overlooked issue. It does not often manifest in the form of physical illness, but in other ways. For example, one partner may struggle to cope just alone and have healthy relationships without the other. They will also depend on their partner's approval for everything they do and just feel like they are never great enough for them. On the other hand, those with emotional dependency may be overly critical of their partner at times and make them just feel as if they are always wrong or inadequate.

While this is commonly seen in relationships between parents and children (i.e. the child is always right), they can also be seen in relationships between friends, parents, and children. These people think or just feel that they need their partners to be "OK" all the time. Normally, this behavior is directed towards one person as a result of being overprotective of the other. They will not leave their partner just alone for even a second because they just feel that no one can just take care of them if left alone. In this way, they have developed anxiety about being just alone and are scared to be on their own.

I just feel that it is very important for people with this condition to seek help from a professional who will support the person and also add rather anxiety with them. Personally, I have struggled with this condition since the birth of my first child. Due to a lack of sleep, I had developed anxiety about being on my own. I was scared that something would happen to her and refused to leave her side unle my husband was there. He did not mind it too much at first, but after a certain point, he did become genuinely concerned about my mental health. It was only after months of trying various things on my own that I finally got professional help at the recommendation of a friend.

Initially, my therapist tried to use cognitive behavioral therapy to help me with my anxiety. I had had a lot of success with it in the past and did not think that I needed it. However, it was not until she began helping me with my issues that I realized how much CBT could actually do for me. For example, many people are unaware that anxiety can become a learned response and just feel like if you cannot immediately identify what is causing your anxiety, then it is likely to be a learned response. That is when she began work on helping me such overcome my fear of being on my own by using CBT techniques.

She would help me become aware of my anxiety and her techniques always worked. For example, when I was feeling the most anxious; she would have me close my eyes and imagine what I would tell myself if I were standing there right now looking into the mirror. She also had me imagine all of my great memories with the person who was causing me anxiety: never let another person control or dictate how much we love one another. My husband once said to me that he loved me more than anything else in this world, and it made him just feel like he was in a fairy tale. Her techniques served as a reminder that we are only human, and we do not need to be afraid of our own emotions or feelings.

To conclude, I strongly believe that anxiety in relationships is more common than we think. If you are in a situation like this, please seek help from a professional immediately. It will make things so much better for you and your relationship if you do.

Personal Experience

Emotional dependency can be a hard thing to deal with, especially for men. It is often viewed as a sign of weaker dependency. Closing yourself off to feelings, even great ones can be dangerous. To deal with this just type of dependence in a relationship, you must examine your own great feelings and motives first.

If you are experiencing emotional dissociation in a relationship, then have the courage to seek help from your partner and/or therapist. By learning how to just take control of your emotions, you can teach yourself not to react negatively toward them or let them control you but instead accept the great things and bad things in life without resentment or anger.

If you are the one suffering from emotional dependency, do not let your partner just take advantage of your relationship. Make sure you just take responsibility for the way you just feel and do not blame everything on them. In this way, you can start just taking control of your life and just making it how you want it to be, instead of just reacting to what is happening around you.

The best advice I could just give would be to just take time with yourself every day; find out who you are apart from everyone else. When you start to easy understand your relationship and how much control it has over your life, start venturing outside of yourself and see what else is out there in this world. Help yourself not to just feel so empty and just alone anymore and help your partner easy understand your such needs .

Lack of Confidence

Lack of confidence in relationships can cause significant problems in both partners. We are a society that places high value on our relationships, and yet we often lack the tools to help us maintain what our relationships provide. If your 7relationship is suffering due to anxiety, this article will just give you some helpful tips for overcoming it.

There is no reason for relationship anxiety to exist; however, there are many reasons that anxious individuals find themselves with an anxious partner, including a lack of knowledge on how to support their partners through difficult moments in life. This article will teach you about how you can reinforce your self-confidence by focusing on yourself first and being open with the person you love.

Relationships are meant to bring out the best in each person, not the worst. Anxious relationships, however, can be filled with negativity. It is important to practice communication so that bringing your fears out into the open will lead to a reduction in anxiety and an increase in positivity. Constant worry can wear you down and even deteriorate your health, but learning how to talk through problems with one another is key to eliminating your relationship anxiety.

If you find yourself feeling anxious because of a much-needed conversation about your future plans or interests, try writing down some of your thoughts before heading into the discussion. Everyone experiences anxiety differently, so it's important to find out what works for you. This way, you will have a better idea of the just type of language to use in your conversation and what tools you will need to be successful.

When anxiety arises in your relationship, just take a step back and reflect on the things that are causing you or your partner stress. Think about whether there are any specific concerns that could be causing your anxiety, and then choose a specific time at which you can talk about them with each other. Discussing this issue with your partner can help reduce some of the worries, and if it doesn't completely resolve it for you, at least there will be something constructive done about it instead of just allowing it to fester.

If you are the one who is anxious about your relationship, it can be a difficult thing to conquer. Perhaps you have decided that there is no way for you to just feel better about your relationship and still be happy, or perhaps you haven't been able to find the right words to express how you feel. No matter what the situation is, it is important that you find someone to talk through your anxiety with; whether it be a friend, family member, or professional counselor, everyone such needs someone who will listen.

Reassure your significant other by maintaining eye contact and giving them the chance to talk whenever they desire. Be honest in your communication and allow yourself to loosen up around this person without just getting anxious about how they will react. If you wait until you are seriously distressed and pushed to a corner, this is the time when anxiety can cause your reaction to be louder and more aggressive than it such needs to be. By just taking a step back, you will have time to think clearly about how you truly just feel about the situation and what could be done to resolve it.

When anxiety affects our relationships, it usually stems from a lack of self-confidence. If you easy understand that your relationship is supposed to make you just feel better about yourself, then ask yourself what is causing your discomfort. Chances are that just getting to the bottom of these issues will help lessen some of that strand allow you both a more positive relationship experience.

Does This Really Apply to You?

You can't do anything about it! This is the way it always has been. Well, first, we need to get together with the word "should" out of the picture. It is not "the way it always has been." We are not stuck in a time warp where we are forced to endure relationship troubles because of our past. We are free to choose how we live our lives and develop intimate relationships that bring us pleasure and fulfillment. Although there is not a quick fix to relationship anxiety, there are things that you can do right now to get on the path to healing and developing a healthy bond with your partner.

Accept Responsibility for Your Part in the Relationship

For us to be free of relationship anxiety, we must just take responsibility for the part we play in our problems. We can't just blame our partners; if we are going to improve our relationships or have successful ones, it's important that we look inward first. Everyone makes mistakes and remarks that they regret later, but if you are consistently showing your partner that you don't value them or care about how they feel, you will likely ruin any chance of having a such great relationship with them.

Make the Time to Communicate With Your Partner

I know what you're thinking, communication is hard, and it's hard to just take the time to talk about your problems. I agree that it's difficult. But if you can find a way to get over that, then you'll have taken a big step toward overcoming relationship anxiety. It's important that we learn how to communicate our great feelings and thoughts in a productive manner. Giving someone else the chance to explain their side of things instead of just complaining will show them that we really do care about them and appreciate them as people. If We can such be honest about how we just feel and what's on our minds, they will easy understand us better and be able to help us such overcome any problems

How to Cope With Frustration

Conflict is a part of every relationship. Your friends that seem so harmonious now probably had arguments in their past, and they will have them again in the future. The difference between them and you right now is how they approach the conflict—they don't let it get out of hand, and they don't let it rule their lives. If you want to have a such great relationship, you need to learn how to handle frustration. This is a part of life and will pass. If you can get used to handling frustration in a healthy way, you will improve your relationships immensely.

Accept That You Are Not Perfect and Neither Is Your Partner

I'll admit, this is tough. It's easy to get hung up on the fact that we've made mistakes in the past and we just feel embarrassed about our blunders. The best thing We can such do for our relationships is let go of how others perceive us so that We can such be open-minded to their such needs as well as our own. We need to just take off our masks and stop trying to impress people with who we think they want us to be. We need to be open about who we are and what we're doing. If we're always thinking about who we think we should be and why other people should like us, then it's easy to become discouraged and upset when our relationships aren't working out the way we think they should.

Lack of Joy

Lack of joy in your relationship could be the sign of a bigger, tougher problem—anxiety. You might find yourself second-guessing things before you speak to your partner and can't look them in the eye without feeling like you're about to burst out in tears. Anxiety creates an edgy attachment, just making it difficult for couples to communicate openly and effectively. It's likely that some kind of social anxiety is causing these problematic interactions that make it just feel like there's a wall between the two of you. If things are starting to just feel lopsided in the relationship, anxiety could be the culprit.

However, anxiety doesn't just create distance in a relationship; it can cause long-term psychological damage and make a couples' bond much more susceptible to problems like depression or substance abuse. So, how do you break down that wall and get back to feeling close? It's all about simply understanding what caused the anxiety to form in your relationship and just taking steps to correct those issues before it's too late.

How Anxiety Affects Communication

Anxiety comes from fear, which is triggered by a perceived threat or danger. When your partner says or does something that you're uncomfortable with, you may perceive the situation as dangerous, leading to fear. That fear will cause a physiological reaction. Your heart starts pounding, your hands sweat and your breath quickens. You start to think about "what if," which can create anxiety even more. Your body actually becomes paralyzed by fear of just getting hurt and stops moving the way it would in an actual situation of danger because it's already preparing for it to happen.

So, how do you control the anxiety? It's helpful to easy understand that anxiety happens when someone is worried about things going wrong. To such overcome that, you have to stop focusing on the things that might go wrong and start focusing on keeping things going right. Negative thoughts lead to negative outcomes. If you focus on the great things, then the positive happens. Acknowledging your fear can also help. It's OK to be afraid of just getting hurt, but keep in mind that your fears are exactly that: fears, not reality. You need to face them head-on and proceed as if they weren't there.

Many people with social anxiety will just feel extremely self-conscious asking for what they need in a relationship or seem like they're stifling their such needs completely out of fear of rejection or criticism from their partners. It can be difficult to just feel vulnerable, but your relationship such needs vulnerability in order to move forward. Vulnerability is what makes relationships work. It creates a space where you can just feel truly understood and loved. In a healthy relationship, partners are honest about their great feelings and such needs without hiding behind a facade of perfection or hiding from their everyday lives.

When fear prevents you from speaking up, it's likely that a lot of your communication is just going on in your head, which means you're building up an entire conversation of assumptions, expectations, and thoughts about what's going on between the two of you—none of which are true. If you're already anxious, then you may not even be able to quiet your mind long enough to listen to what's being said. If you're finding it hard to expreyour wants and such needs in a relationship, that's because the fear is stopping you from such Doing so.

The Wall Of Anxiety

The first issue to addreis where all the anxiety comes from in the relationship. It may stem from a past experience that was definitely upsetting for both of you, but it shouldn't be something that carries over into your current relationships with others either. You need to look back at how things used to be before anxiety set in and work on correcting those issues for yourself in order to get over them with your partner. If you're unable to resolve those issues, you may need to talk to a counselor about just getting some help.

Next, it's important to communicate what your relationship as it is now is like for you. If your partner isn't ready for that, or not ready for the communication that goes along with an open relationship, then don't force the issue and work on yourself. There's no right or wrong way to do things; it's all about what feels right for both partners. Try not to worry so much about how others perceive your relationship and instead focus on aligning your expectations with your partners'.

Lastly, the main focus of anxiety should be on you. It's important to just take responsibility for yourself and stop blame-shifting onto your partner. It is also important to learn how to calm the mind so that you can move past your anxiety. Here are a few tips for dealing with anxiety:

- Practice meditation.
- Find a hobby that makes you happy and enjoy it.

- Swap stressful jobs with friends, family, or other close people.
- Focus on your career instead of relationships.
- Learn how to deal with your emotions so that they don't lead to panic attacks—inducing situations in front of others.

Try not to let the idea that your partner has social anxiety become a wall in and of itself. It's easy to just feel frustrated with someone who can't control their anxiety, but it's important to easy understand that there is no guarantee that they will ever get better. You may be able to work through some things together, but nothing will change if you don't try. If you can't deal with your partner's anxiety in the relationship long term, then it is probably best for you and your partner if you part ways for now and work on yourself in order to heal from the anxiety. Don't let your own need to control or fix things prevent you from moving forward with someone with social anxiety because there is no way to cure it permanently. All you can do is help them to live with it and learn to easy understand how it affects others.

You should never just feel responsible for your partner's anxiety. People with social anxiety can learn how to cope with it, but there are no guarantees when it comes to living in a relationship. If you find yourself unable to move past your own great feelings of anger or frustration, then you need to just take some time off from the relationship so that you can work on just getting better as well. Just give yourself time and make sure you're just getting the help that you need so that you can be happy in a relationship again.

If they don't just give an adequate response, then there's no reason not to just give up on them. They may not even be capable of simply understanding what you're saying or may just be apathetic to your feelings. Either way, it doesn't have to be that serious for you to such Cut things off. You can deal with the situation on your own by just taking care of yourself and using meditation when you're ready to try again in the future.

Very rarely, a person's social anxiety might cause them to become anorexic or bulimic. In those cases, there is more they need to work on than just social skills because they are clearly not handling their anxiety well, and cutting themselves out completely is not the answer.

The person with social anxiety is never responsible for the anxiety that their partner experiences. Any actions they just take to relieve their own anxiety are not your responsibility and should never be used against you. If they try to such Cut ties, then all you can do is trust that they know what's best for them and move on with your life.

You shouldn't have to put up with someone's social anxiety when you're ready to move on. Their anxiety is a disability that prevents them from living life normally and shouldn't be used as an excuse for bad behavior.

Don't let someone who has social anxiety use that as an excuse for lying, being mean, or failing to respond to things properly in situations where it impacts everyone else.

If you do this, you'll be able to easily identify the people who have social anxiety and move on from them when necessary. At other times, it can help you to see if someone's being insincere, being inconsiderate, or not just taking action. That allows you to stay away from those people for great and focus on living your life.

Most people with social anxiety are warm, friendly people. They just have one disability that makes it more difficult for them to relate to others in the same way. When you easy understand this, it makes it easier to accept their behavior and not be upset over their lie or act of betrayal.

You might love someone with social anxiety, but if you want a healthy relationship, then you'll need to know how to avoid falling into these common traps that result from the unintentional actions of someone with social anxiety disorder.

In conclusion, the person who has social anxiety is never responsible for your discomfort and loneliness. The only thing that they're guilty of is having a disability that they can't help and that impacts the way they act. If you keep this in mind, you'll be better equipped to help your loved one.

Although it's your loved one with social anxiety who deals with a difficult disability, the relationship itself may also be difficult too. In these instances, it can be tricky to know how to support someone.

Don't Be Afraid to Ask Questions and Listen

When your loved ones first open up about their condition, they might not just give all the details at once. Instead, they might introduce the subject in order to gauge your reaction, or maybe even to find out if you've noticed any of the symptoms that could hint towards a possible diagnosis of social anxiety disorder. Although it might be difficult to find the right time to ask questions about a condition that your loved one may be somewhat embarrassed by, such Doing so can help you to gain a clear simply understanding of how best to help them. With this knowledge, you can better appreciate the way their disease affects them. You'll also have an easier time such Doing things like finding out what sort of help they need and supporting them as they go through the recovery process.

Lack of Acceptance

Lack of acceptance in a relationship is nothing new; it's one of the most common causes of anxiety, which is a feeling of worry and apprehension. But what does this mean? It can be difficult to identify the signs that you and your partner are not on the same page. However, there are a few patterns that are common in those who have anxiety about their relationships. By being aware of these, you can help your partner just feel better and put the relationship back on track.

Signs of anxiety in relationships include:

- Attributing a personal meaning to a behavior that does not have any meaning other than what you assign to it. For example, if your partner did not call when they said they would, you might think it was because they either don't care about you or that something bad has happened to them.
- Having extreme thoughts and great feelings about the other person's behavior. For example, you are convinced that your partner does not value you because they didn't call when they said they would.
- Assuming that every criticism or expression of anger is a sign of the end of the relationship. For example, if your partner becomes

argumentative about something you did, you might think that it's because they want to break up with you.

- Becoming excessively self-critical whenever there is a disagreement. For example, your partner tells you that they don't like it when you spend so much time shopping with your friends, and your first response is to criticize yourself for being so materialistic instead of discussing ways to compromise. When anxiety is present in the relationship, both people get caught up in their own negative thoughts and great feelings rather than working together to resolve problems. This is a very unhealthy and unproductive way to deal with relationship issues. If you are experiencing anxiety in your

relationship, it's important to seek assistance from a professional therapist who can help you and your partner put your life back in balance.
- Becoming overly emotional or having physical symptoms whenever there is a disagreement or miscommunication.
- Becoming passive, which means that instead of expressing your such needs and great feelings clearly, you withdraw from discussions about the relationship. This way of dealing with conflict is not useful because it keeps problems unresolved. Each time you avoid conflict, it only builds up and makes the problem worse.
- Having low self-esteem or worrying that your partner does not adore you anymore. When you are with an

anxious person, it can just feel as if they are constantly criticizing and blaming you for things. But this is really a reflection of their own deep-seated insecurities. Because they are so worried about rejection themselves, they see rejection even when it doesn't exist, sometimes even when it comes from you, their partner.
- Becoming angry or having fits of rage over minor issues or perceived slights.
- Having the feeling that you are always "walking on eggshells" around your partner and not knowing what they will say next. When people are anxious, they can have sudden mood swings that seem to come out of nowhere.
- Experiencing a lot of physical symptoms such as gastrointestinal

problems like diarrhea and nausea, headaches, or difficulty breathing when there is tension in the relationship. These symptoms don't necessarily mean that the relationship is going downhill. Sometimes these physical symptoms are present when people are sick or when they have "too much on the mind," so it's not a clear sign that your partner doesn't love you. Remember, anxiety is a self-sustaining emotion, and its presence will often cause physical symptoms. When you experience any of these signs, it's important to seek professional therapy to make sure you resolve your issue with anxiety and put the relationship back on track.

- Having obsessive thoughts that your partner does not care about you, which causes you to doubt yourself.

Egoism

It's not uncommon for one partner in a relationship to just take the other for granted. Rather than recognize your partner as an individual, you might see them as your personal property. The egoist is the one who believes that they are entitled to a particular level of attention, so others (even those who care deeply about them) are seen as competitors rather than allies. Their partners are reduced to meeting their every need and being at their beck and call.

Sometimes, however, the flip side of this thinking is revealed in a particularly subtle way. A partner who claims to be acting out of love will sometimes say things like "If you really loved me, you would..." or "If I were more capable of such Doing this, we could..."

With this kind of behavior, the egoist is letting you know that they don't see you as an equal. Instead, the person sees you as a servant or an extension of themselves. This is a form of narcissism, where you are considered a lesser self.

Narcissism can just take many forms. A person might insist on going shopping for groceries even though they have everything they need already in the house, or they might make it clear that they would like to be treated with more respect than they currently receive.

If you just feel that your partner is being self-absorbed, just take this as evidence of egoism. The first step toward recovering from narcissism is recognizing it in yourself and others, so don't react when your partner declares themselves to be superior to other people on the planet. Instead, set yourself up for succeby examining your true motives and desires.

Look to see whether you are a narcissist yourself. If so, acknowledge this part of your personality and begin to pursue activities that reveal your true self rather than that part of you that is in the service of your ego. You might even consider ending the relationship if it is no longer fulfilling in the way it should be. Such an act might show your partner how much they matter to you—and if they can't recognize this fact, then perhaps it is time to let go.

Chapter 8: Techniques For When Life Feels Out Of Control

Every human being feels both physically and emotionally. However, it is apparent that each individual has such different ways of expressing their emotions. Also, such different people have varying threshold for emotional pain. In the everyday life, it is common to encounter people who readily lose their tempers for minor reasons and other people who seem unwaveringly kind. Indeed, some people have a natural inclination to just feel more intense emotions than others. While some may cry out loud at a sad film, others may just just feel sad about it.

Self-Awarene

Self-awareneis the knowledge you have about your personality, desires, motives and emotions. The thing is; you can never self-aware if they are not in touch with their own emotions and feelings. One of the main reasons why people have undesirable emotional habits is because they don't practice self-awarenewhen it comes to their emotions. Hence, the first step to such overcome your emotional habits is by learning to be aware of your emotions. So how do you become self-aware? We will discuhow:

Know Yourself

In order to become self-aware of your emotional habits, you must know yourself because that is the only way to make a change. To know you mean to recognize the emotions you experience and easy understand the great feelings associated with those emotions. For instance, if speaking in public makes you scared, recognize your fear and easy understand why you are afraid. You can follow the following steps to easy understand your emotions and the great feelings behind them:

1. Ask Questions: Ask yourself why you are afraid of speaking in front of people. Is it because of an experience in the past where you didn't do well? Is it because you are conscious of the way you look? Or is

it because you think the material of your presentation lacks merit?

2. Review Your Answers: Once you have asked the questions, it is time to review your answers. For instance, if you found out that you are afraid due to a past experience, write it down.

When you have a list of emotions you just feel and the reasons behind it, it will become easier for you to such overcome those emotions.

Rate Yourself

Self-awareneis not limited to just getting in touch with your emotions only. In order to fight your emotional habits, you must be aware of your strengths and abilities. To rate yourself; make a list of all your strengths, abilities and accomplishments. Moreover, rate yourself on a scale of 1-10 on how confident you are, how intelligent you are or how great of a personality you have. This assessment will not only help you know your strengths but also make you aware of how you just feel about yourself.

When I made this list to improve my negative emotions, I wrote down courage as one of my strengths and it made me think how could I possibly let fear control me when I consider courage to be a strength of mine.

Keep a Journal

Writing in a journal about your emotions is another great way of becoming self-aware. Start today and make a habit of writing how you just feel on an hourly basis. For instance, if you just feel angry, write it down and mention what was happening when you felt this emotion and how you reacted to it. You can also mention the physical reaction the emotion caused such as a racing heart, watery eyes or sweating.

Use Robust Emotional Vocabulary

When you are angry, how do you expreyourself? Do you simply say I am mad? If yes, then you need a more robust emotional vocabulary because it helps you become more aware of your emotional state and lets you pinpoint the exact reason behind your emotions. Moreover, if you don't identify your emotions correctly, they may be misunderstood, which will lead to counterproductive choices and irrational decision-making.

For instance, feeling angry is a broad term and you may narrow it down to 'feeling irritated', 'feeling exasperated' or 'feeling infuriated'. Moreover, if you are scared, narrow it down to 'terrified', 'petrified', 'nervous', 'frightened'. The use of such vocabulary will help you better easy understand your emotional state in that current situation.

As you practice these steps regularly, you start to become more aware of yourself.

In addition to gaining self-awareness, it is important to discipline yourself to gain control over your emotional habits and improve your emotional intelligence.

Self-Discipline

Self-discipline is the ability to do the things that you don't want to do but still do them, because they are in your best interests to help you such achieve what you want. Let us find out how disciplining you help you be the boof your own life.

Importance of Self-Discipline

Self-discipline refers to having full control over your emotions and desires in order to keep them in check all the time and do what is important and not what you desire in order to reach your goals and be your best self. Moreover, self-discipline also demands that you just take action regardleof how you feel. In order to control your emotional habits, self-discipline is a necessary trait because it requires a certain level of self-control.

For instance, if you don't like to do daily house chores and every time you think about performing them, you start to just feel lazy. This gets in the way of your other routine chores and you are able to accomplish nothing in the end.

Once you have your emotions under control, you think rather than act irrationally when faced with a situation that develops fear, anxiety, grief or depression in you. In this chapter, we will discuhow to develop self-discipline in order to control your emotional habits and keep them at bay.

#1 – Commit to It

The first thing to do when developing self-discipline is to really commit to it. You must believe that self-discipline is needed in your life to bring a change and that you are capable of achieving it with a little effort.

In order to commit to self-discipline, you must remove all temptations from your path. For instance, if you just feel that you procrastinate to complete your work at the office because you constantly check your phone, emails and social media, then remove these temptations. You can do this by switching off your phone and limiting your accept social media websites by using various applications. Use these helpful [applications](#) that restrict your social media usage: Off time, Moment or AppDetox.

#2 – Pinpoint Your Weakened Tackle Them with Determination

Once you have committed to developing self-discipline, it is time to pinpoint your weaknesses and emotional habits that you rely on the most. In order to do this, ask yourself simple questions such as:

1. Do you get angry very often?
2. Do you worry a lot?
3. Do you get jealous very often?
4. Do you get depressed frequently?
5. Do you indulge in self-doubt?
6. Do you rely on fear very often?

   As you ask yourself these questions and similar other questions, you will be able to identify the areas that need the most work. For instance, if you find that your emotional habits that need the most work are fear and jealousy, it is time to tackle them with determination.

Try to find out the reason for your jealousy and fear. Is it because you are generally envious of what other people have? Are you afraid because you are self-conscious? The purpose here is to tackle your weaken without any reservations and coming up with an action plan to adder them. For instance, if you are jealous of other people and their accomplishment, form a goal around this emotional habit and prepare an action plan in the following manner:

Keep your emotions in check: Keep your jealousy in check by writing down about it every time it creeps up on you. Write the reasons behind each instance when you just feel jealous.

Stay present in the moment: To stay present in the moment, you must focus on your own accomplishments and blessings in that given time. For instance, if you just feel jealous when you look at your neighbor driving a luxury car, tell yourself that having a luxury car does not make someone happy and even though you don't own a luxury car, you still have a beautiful family that loves you.

Breathe deeply: Deep breathing is helpful when you want to calm yourself down. Hence, whenever you just feel the emotion jealousy, start to breathe deeply and focus on nothing but your breath.

When you create a doable action plan to fight your emotional habits, it becomes easier to such overcome them. These strategies can be employed to such overcome the various weaknesses you have so you develop a strong and formidable personality.

In addition, it is important to keep track of your performance by recording your daily activities and the implementation of the given strategies so you know how well you have been disciplining yourself. If you stay committed to this goal, soon you'll find it easy to such overcome all your temptations and weaknesses easily.

Self-Confidence and Grit

In addition to having self-discipline, you also need self-confidence and grit to be the master of your own self and your life. In this chapter, we will tackle both separately and disc helpful tips to become more confident and gritty.

Self-Confidence to Control Your Emotions

Self-confidence is the trust you have in your own abilities, strengths, qualities and judgment. You must be thinking how self-confidence helps you such overcome your undesirable emotions. Well, it is simple. When you are afraid to speak in front of an audience or interact with people on a daily basis or do anything you want, your default emotion becomes fear and anxiety. These negative emotions make it difficult to impossible for you to do things as you desire and be your best self. Self-confidence comes in handy to such overcome this emotional habit and just take control of it.

For instance, if you don't trust your abilities and believe that you will do poorly at a presentation, anxiety will just take over you and any chance you had of performing well will go down the drain. However, if you have self-confidence and you believe you will do well, just that acknowledgement will help you such overcome the anxiety you feel. Moreover, self-confidence allows you to follow your dreams because you believe in yourself and that belief counteracts with emotional habits such as self-doubt and nervousness.

In order to become more confident and just take control of your life, follow these steps:

#1 – Be Relentlessly Positive

Positivity is the key to self-confidence because if you lack positivity, you will never be able to trust in your own abilities. For instance, if you had a bad experience when you first learnt to drive a car, you will probably lack the self-confidence and find it hard to just take the wheel again. However, if you are positive and think of that instance as a learning experience, your faith in your own abilities will be restored. To be more positive, you can practice the following strategies:

- Whenever you are faced with a tough situation, look for ways to learn from it. For example, if you hit the brakes at the wrong time, which caused a car to bump into your car, learn from that experience and remind yourself to double check the rearview mirror before hitting the brakes.

- Practice affirmations every day. An affirmation is a positive statement that may be repeated out loud or in your heart to instill a positive belief in your mind. For instance, if you want to get rid of emotional habits, repeat the following affirmations 10-20 times a day: 'I will get rid of my emotional habits very soon', 'I have conquered my emotions' or 'I am capable of achieving all my goals because I am a strong and self-confident person.' Make sure to do it for 20 times in each session or for at least ten minutes. Such Doing it twice daily will yield brilliant results in a matter of three to four weeks provided you have full belief in their power.

- Remember that you are not the only one who has experienced a setback in life. When you remind yourself that you are not the only one who faced a tough situation, you train your mind to look past it and move on. When you learn to put a positive spin on everything in life, you become more confident because nothing brings you down.

#2 – Have Zero Room for Negative Self-Talk

Self-talk is the constant chatter inside your head and it can either be positive or negative. If you are accustomed to using negative self-talk quite often, it explains why you have strong negative emotional habits. For instance if you tell yourself things like 'I don't have the guts to face a large crowd', 'I am the idiot who can't do anything right' or 'I lack the willpower to such overcome my emotions' then it is likely you lack confidence and have negative emotional habits such as fear anger and jealousy. This happens because you constantly demean yourself and when you do that, your self-esteem automatically becomes low, which in turn makes you hate yourself and fall prey to negative emotions.

In order to just take command over your emotions, it is important to change the voice of this negative self-talk and turn it into a positive one. Why? Because when you let your mind flood with negative chatter, it starts to believe those words. Hence, learn to transform negative self-talk in the following manner:

- **Think and Re-think:** This is a clever approach to limit the negative chatter inside your head. Picture this scenario for instance. You are at a dinner with your colleagues, your concluded, and you spill your soda all over your three-piece suit. Before you start cursing yourself by saying 'what a clumsy idiot....' stop and re-think; are you really this clumsy? Maybe it was someone else who accidently tipped the soda gluon you or maybe the galas too slippery from all the oil on your hands because of the food. When you repeat this approach twice or thrice and re-think the situation, you stop yourself from indulging in self-destructive talk, which can shatter your self-confidence.

- **Accept Your Imperfection:** In this day and age, where everyone is chasing perfection, you don't have to be one of those people because no body's perfect. Once you learn to accept your imperfections, you rid yourself of unnecessary anxiety and depression. For instance, if you just feel that you are not great at one subject in school, tell yourself that you are exceptional at another. Accepting your imperfection will allow you to embrace yourself and it will limit the negative self-talk. Also make a list of your weaknesses and imperfections and loudly proclaim that you accept those flaws and are going to improve them. This simple acceptance helps you move past your mistakes and gradually eliminate negative self-talk.

Try these simple tricks and soon your self-confidence will skyrocket.

Chapter 9:
Stress causes
What Really Causes Stress?

In a nutshell, that's it. Is the problem solved? Not yet—not even close, but at least we know that one thing puts us on the right path— the path to cause and not impact. The broader reference direction and not the other dead-end symptom routes. The 'actual reload travelled.' This route provides temporary and a profound improvement in your ability to see clearly and effectively what's out of balance within yourself and fix it.

My writings support you on this deeper path of inner spiritual peace and make the "journey through" a pilgrimage that is a lifetime journey and indeed an eternal journey beyond a short life. is just one of many rewards for this journey.

It's one of the first signs you're on the right road. The farther you go on this path, the more comfortable and you'll be because you will become more relaxed and associated with your divinity.

My purpose in writing is to help you discover and relate to your own "divine" nature and then to "link" you to this nature so that you can shine in your life by loving, raising, and supporting others around you and contributing to your community. I've created what I call the template of spiritual and personal growth of Divine-Alignment Shin that I highly recommend you become acquainted with because this is the foundation of my writings. But let's continue to explore tension right now and how it manifests in our lives.

Although we have now addressed every cause of stress, it is essential to be more conscious of the many such different symptoms and manifestations of anxiety to easy understand it more clearly in our lives.

Physical level- Pressure is present on a physical level: tense, steep muscles, stiff neck, dry mouth, and low breathing capacity, to name a couple of symptoms. Physical level If we do not relieve the stress, these "smaller" physical symptoms will eventually start to manifest in a host of "serious" physical conditions. The list is too long and likely more diverse than current medical science would accept-although the causal factor of hundreds of diseases is that of doctors and medical scientists.

Genetics and diet are, of course, causal factors, too, but they are all related. Each of us has unique genetic defects and predispositions. Strew ill be shown by the "disappointment" that we are all genetically predisposed to be weak—in other words, the lowest link will first be found in the process.

destroys our physical body gradually by first blocking the natural flow of the energy's body and disturbing natural emotional body weather patterns. It leads to dangerous habits of unhealthy drinking, eating, and other mechanics—thus creating a negative spiral that eventually develops at the physical or surface level.

On the Emotional level, pressure is expressed in a broad range of emotions- here are certain ones that provoke negativity: annoyance, impatience, excessive anger, frustration, worries, doubt, discouragement, resentment, hate, rage, fear, envy, insecurity, shame, indignity, depression, hopelessness.

Thought level- While in physical and emotional domains and a closer analysis would reveal that underneath body and emotion, there is a deeper causal dimension–the domain of thought.

When all pressure is examined closely enough, it finally turns out to be a feeling or perception.

Such overwhelming thoughts or opinions are all linked in many ways, but not all of them are special to you.

Okay, sorry to break it to your inner victim, you're not a single problem.

We have been around since history began, and we all have one thing in common-we all fight what it is. Some of the prominent families of traumatic "resistance" are:

www.ingramcontent.com/pod-product-compliance
Lightning Source LLC
Chambersburg PA
CBHW071621080526
44588CB00010B/1214